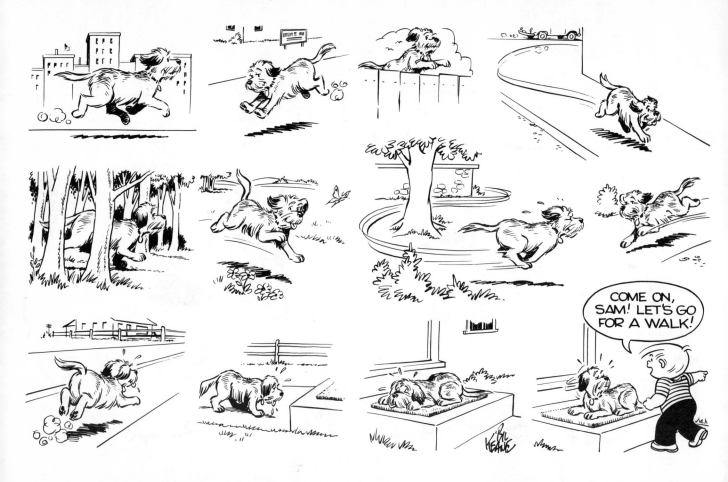

Seven-year-old Billy helps Daddy out by providing this sampling of his own cartoons.

Dolly Pulling her Hare Out

PJ's Rocking the Boat

These are Jeffy's

Son Glasses

This is a Stick Cup!

Daddy Taking his Pick

A Belt in the Mouth

Dolly has appeal

Mommy I need my Shirt and Pants!

A Clothes Call for Jeffy

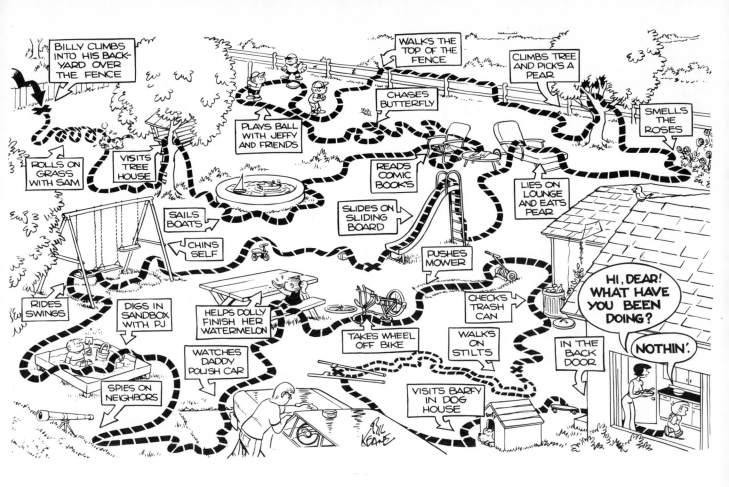

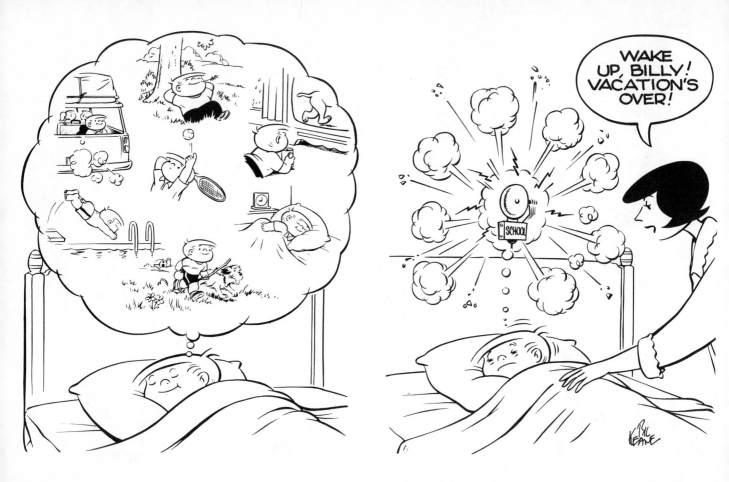

FIRST DOWN

SCREEN PLAY

UNNECESSARY ROUGHNESS

SUBSTITUTIONS

TWO MINUTE WARNING

GETTING READY TO KICK

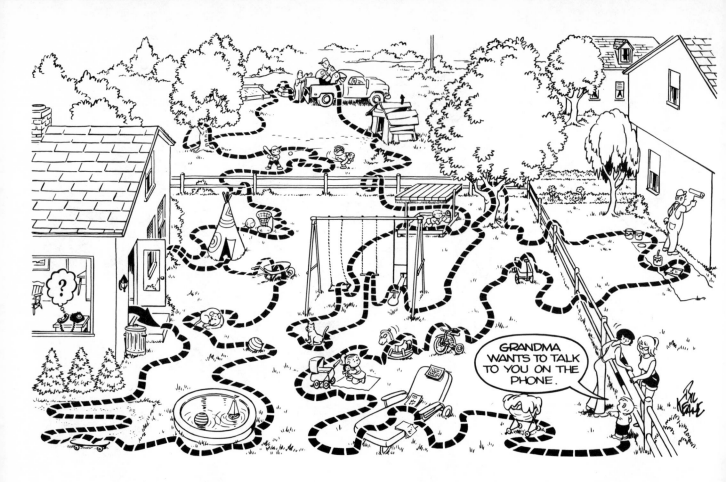

GUEST ARTIST BILLY (AGE 7) DEPICTS HOW DADDY DRAWS A FAMILY CIRCUS CARTOON.

TRIES to think of an idea

Tries to dream up an idea on the couch

Stares out window

Maybe reading a book will help

Still can't think of anything

Suddenly idea strikes!

Here, Billy, let's see what you can do.

Son Billy does a GREAT Job